INCREDIBLE INVENTORS

THOMAS EDISON AND THE LIGHT BULB

BY BENJAMIN PROUDFIT

Gareth Stevens
PUBLISHING

Please visit our website, www.garethstevens.com. For a free color catalog of all our high-quality books, call toll free 1-800-542-2595 or fax 1-877-542-2596.

Library of Congress Cataloging-in-Publication Data

Names: Proudfit, Benjamin, author.
Title: Thomas Edison and the light bulb / Benjamin Proudfit.
Description: New York : Gareth Stevens Publishing, [2023] | Series: Incredible inventors | Includes index.
Identifiers: LCCN 2021036664 (print) | LCCN 2021036665 (ebook) | ISBN 9781538276624 (set) | ISBN 9781538276631 (library binding) | ISBN 9781538276617 (paperback) | ISBN 9781538276648 (ebook)
Subjects: LCSH: Edison, Thomas A. (Thomas Alva), 1847-1931–Juvenile literature. | Inventors–United States–Biography–Juvenile literature. | Electrical engineers–United States–Biography–Juvenile literature.
Classification: LCC TK140.E3 P77 2023 (print) | LCC TK140.E3 (ebook) | DDC 621.3092 [B]–dc23
LC record available at https://lccn.loc.gov/2021036664
LC ebook record available at https://lccn.loc.gov/2021036665

Published in 2023 by
Gareth Stevens Publishing
111 East 14th Street, Suite 349
New York, NY 10003

Designer: Rachel Rising
Editor: Kristen Nelson

Photo credits: Cover, p. 1 [Thomas Alva Edison]/Libary of Congress; pp. 3-24 Zavadskyi Ihor/Shutterstock.com; pp. 3-24 Lukasz Szwaj/Shuttesrstock.com; p. 5 Everett Collection/Shutterstock.com; p. 7 Jirik V/Shutterstock.com; p. 9 https://commons.wikimedia.org/wiki/File:EdisonPhonograph.jpg; p. 11 https://commons.wikimedia.org/wiki/File:Menlo_Park_Laboratory.JPG; pp. 13, 20 Morphart Creation/Shutterstock.com; p. 15 serpi/Shutterstock.com; p.17 https://commons.wikimedia.org/wiki/File:Brockton_Edison.jpg; p. 19 VK Studio/Shutterstock.com.

Printed in the United States of America

CPSIA compliance information: Batch #CSGS23: For further information contact Gareth Stevens, New York, New York at 1-800-542-2595.

CONTENTS

Boldface words appear in the glossary.

Early Life

Thomas Edison is one of the greatest inventors in American history. He was born February 11, 1847, in Ohio. Thomas didn't go to school for long. His mother taught him at home. He liked to read and do **experiments**.

Thomas got his first job on a railroad in 1859. Soon after, he lost most of his hearing. Then, in 1862, he learned how to use a **telegraph**. He became so good at it that he spent years working with the telegraph all over the country.

TELEGRAPH

Inventor and More

By the late 1860s, Thomas began working as a full-time inventor. He made the telegraph, and later the telephone, better. This work led to his invention of the **phonograph** in 1877. The next year, he began work on **electric** lights.

PHONOGRAPH

Menlo Park

In the late 1870s, Thomas founded a lab in Menlo Park, New Jersey. Here, he and his scientists worked to make a light bulb safe to use in homes. They wanted it to be able to stay lit for a long time too.

MENLO PARK

The Light Bulb Moment

Thomas wasn't the first inventor to work on electric lighting. In 1802, Humphry Davy had invented the electric arc lamp. However, it didn't burn for long and was too bright. People invented other light bulbs too. None were **practical** enough to be sold to the public.

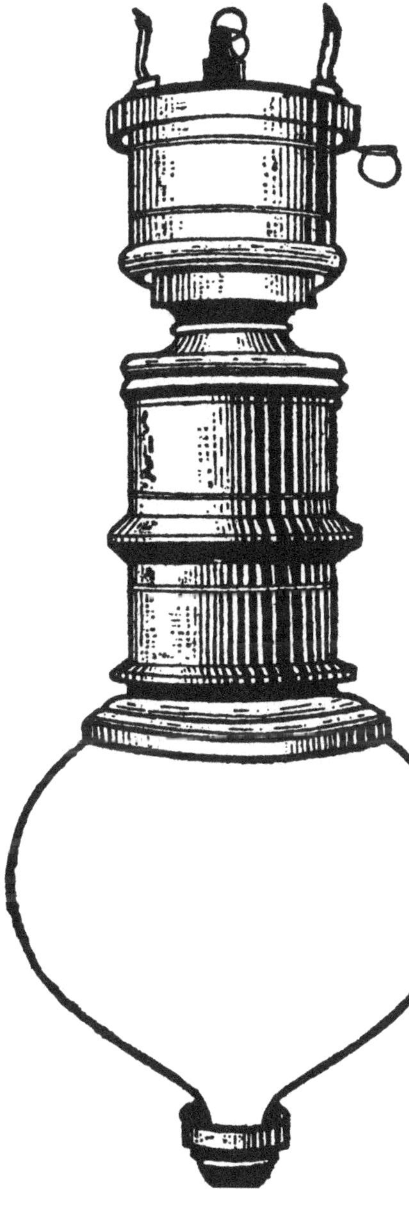

ELECTRIC ARC LAMP

Thomas solved the problems of past light bulbs. He found the right **material** for the **filament**. It could burn for many hours and was safe for use in homes. Thomas received a **patent** for this light bulb in 1880.

EDISON'S LIGHT BULB

The light bulb was just the beginning. Thomas invented a whole electric lighting **system**! He used electric light for his lab in Menlo Park and showed the public in late 1879. In 1882, the first **commercial** power station opened in New York City.

EDISON POWER STATION, 1883, BROCKTON, MASSACHUSETTS

Music and Movies

Following his success with the electric light, Thomas began to work on the phonograph again. He improved it enough for use in homes and businesses. It could play music! Thomas was also part of inventions that led to the movie business.

The End of Invention

The way Thomas used his laboratories to work on ideas and inventions was different from the ways of earlier inventors. His way of inventing may have been his best invention! During his life, this incredible inventor received 1,093 patents. He died October 18, 1931.

TIMELINE

February 11, 1847
Thomas Edison is born in Ohio.

1862
He learns to use the telegraph.

1877
He invents the phonograph.

1879
Menlo Park is lit with electric lighting for the public to see.

1880
Thomas receives a patent for his electric light bulb.

1882
The first commercial electric power station opens in New York City.

October 18, 1931
Thomas Edison dies.

GLOSSARY

commercial: having to do with the buying and selling of goods and services

electric: having to do with electricity, or the flow of electrical power

experiment: a scientific test in which someone carries out a series of actions and watches what happens in order to learn about something

filament: a single thread or a thin, threadlike object. In a light bulb, this is the part that lights up when electricity moves through it.

material: a type of matter

patent: an official document that gives a person the rights to a design, machine, or process for a time

phonograph: a kind of old-fashioned record player

practical: having to do with what is real and possible

system: a group of similar parts that move or work together

telegraph: a method of communicating using electric signals sent through wires

FOR MORE INFORMATION

BOOKS

Boone, Mary. *Thomas Edison: Physicist and Inventor.* Oxford, UK: Raintree, 2019.

Raatma, Lucia. *Thomas Edison: The Man Behind the Light Bulb.* North Mankato, MN: Pebble, 2020.

WEBSITES

Kids & Youth - Thomas Edison National Historical Park

www.nps.gov/edis/learn/kidsyouth/index.htm

Read more about Thomas Edison and the time he lived in.

Thomas Edison for Kids | DK Find Out

www.dkfindout.com/us/science/famous-scientists/thomas-edison/

Explore many famous scientists, including Thomas Edison, here.

INDEX